Master What Matters: The Power of Your Vision ~ Seven Keys to Unlocking It

Henry O. Vero

Table of Contents

Chapter 1

Knowing and understanding your vision:

Understanding your vision entails being aware of who you are (your purpose), where you're heading (your vision for the future), and the principles you'll need to use to steer your course (your values).

Consider your vision as your North Star, leading the way anytime you become lost in the hustle and bustle of daily life. It helps you see clearly into the future while focusing on the here and now. A lack of vision keeps you from experiencing achievement or importance in life.

"If you are focused on your goals, you are less likely to get sidetracked by the many options and competing agendas that may otherwise detour you." Timothy Gallwey

Vision: Three Components

The purpose is the first of the three components. You exist for a reason, which is your mission. Your mission as a person is what drives you. Understanding what industry you are in is the goal for firms. A purpose isn't concerned with the person or the company. It's all about contributing value and making a difference instead.

vision for the future is the second component. Visualizing your ideal future with clarity is essential. You need to be very clear about your goals and where you're headed. Visualize desired results and situations.

The third component, fundamental values, provides you with the instruments you need to direct your choices and activities. Your conduct is shaped by these principles, which also help you choose the proper course of action. Discipline, honesty, and integrity are a few examples of values.

The mission of Vision

Having a vision is different from just wanting something. You can't just wish for success to come into your life. need to have a vision that motivates you to go beyond what you already know and have achieved. To create a compelling vision of the future, is the goal of vision.

The most successful individuals in the world have concise vision statements that help them stay focused on what is most important. For this reason, having a life vision is essential.

Take a look at Sir Richard Branson's mission statement:

"To enjoy life as I go through it and learn from my errors."

The mission statement of Oprah Winfrey also states:

"I want to teach. And to be renowned for pushing my pupils to achieve more than they ever imagined they were capable of. You may concentrate on your vision, future, and values by having a vision statement. You must express your vision in writing, no matter what it is.

Your Vision: A Guide

Please respond to the questions below to help us understand your vision.

Determine your life's purpose.

What motivates you?

Describe your talents.

What motivates you?

What interests you deeply?

Be aware of your destination.

In five, ten, or twenty years, where do you see yourself?

Which future do you want to have?

Establish your essential principles.

What values are essential for achieving your objectives?

What ethics or moral standards do you need to study to get there?

The Power of Your Vision: Seven Keys to Unlocking It

1. Vision is exposed to the listener in a listening posture.

You must spend some time alone with God and pay attention to His instructions in order to unleash the power of your vision. The living room after everyone has gone to bed, a stroll in the early morning, or a secluded area in the park may all serve as your space. Your undisturbed time with Him must be spent alone. Tell your loved ones not to bother you and put away your mobile gadgets, TV, Facebook page, and other electronic devices.

2. Vision must be recorded in writing.

Write down what God tells you after you've prayed and sought Him out for some time. It should be written in the present tense, as though it has already occurred. Your target location's coordinates and the proper instructions to take to get there are provided in a written vision. It provides you with the inspiration and drive you need in order to overcome the hardest obstacles in life.

3. The vision must be clear.

You must express your vision in clear, uncomplicated terms that even a fifth-grader can comprehend. Clearing out any uncertainty that can get in the way of your success by developing an easy-to-understand vision is beneficial. A simple vision will energise and stoke enthusiasm in everyone who is linked to it, and they will follow it with eager expectation.

4. A vision posting is required.

It is now time to submit your vision so that everyone involved may read it once you have clearly expressed it in writing. The vision statement you've placed serves as a continual reminder of the possibilities for your life, family, and/or marriage if you follow its instructions. It becomes your inspiration to overcome the setbacks, diversion, and disappointments in life that obstruct your goals.

5. Vision gets beyond obstacles.

Do not assume that because God gives you a precise vision, everything will happen without a hitch. You will face some significant obstacles, as well as unanticipated turmoil. However, when God gives you a vision, He gives you the strength and bravery to follow it and the offensive offensive assault that will enable you to conquer any barrier that lies in your way.

6. The vision will come to pass in God's timing.

Please take your time focusing. Do not rush. Making your own plans to realize your vision forces those goals into your own schedule, which may postpone or veer your destiny. When God judges the proper moment, visions come to pass.

7. Faith is required to live a vision.

Your faith develops as you give more of yourself to your goal. The door to success is opened by taking little, steady steps in the direction of your objective. You will fearlessly go ahead in pursuing your promised path that leads to the realization of your vision if you decide to activate your faith.

If you put these seven points into practice, your vision will have a significant influence on your life, your family, and everyone you are related to.

Chapter 2

State the fact about your life

Successful people use their brain's power to intelligently build their realities and the outcomes they desire in life. They genuinely think they can accomplish anything they put their minds to.

They have confidence in themselves despite their current situation. Because they are surrounded by inspiring people, exclusively discuss their desires in life, and consume only good news, they attract extraordinary events.

The rest of civilization, on the other hand, encloses itself within four walls.

Every idea is a source of pain, replaying depressing tales and speaking the same lines like a record that is constantly playing. Stories that show the world how scarce they are, how they moan, and how they choose to place the responsibility for their general lack of success on others.

I would love to share some amazing information with you regarding your brain. Dr. Joe Dispenza's book Evolve Your Brain:

The Science of Changing Your Mind contains these statistics.

1. An unknown amount of neurochemicals, which are necessary for the proper functioning of your nervous system, are released by your brain with each thought through an upsurge in electrical currents.
Your body reacts to each idea in the appropriate way, acting as if you were a famous symphony under the direction of a master conductor, with your heart, liver, and lungs all playing their parts precisely.

2. Our neural wiring is shaped by the things we pay attention to in life—what, where, how, and for how long—as well as by our recurring ideas.

3. When you focus on physical pain, electrical currents are sent from your body to your mind, which keeps the suffering coming.

4. Repeated thoughts establish anchored neural connections in the brain.
These ideas transition between conscious and unconscious modes of thinking and being.
On auto-pilot, that is how we behave.

5. The process of change necessitates letting go of what we already know to learn new ways of being.
Regular meditation practice speeds up the completion of this task and yields observable favorable outcomes.

6. It takes a lot of effort and our whole focus to learn something new. Think about how attentive you were when you first learned to drive a car compared to an experienced driver who largely drives on auto-pilot. Every new piece of knowledge we discover has the potential to change who we are. A new experience is created by fusing this new knowledge with real-world application. The

more often this procedure is repeated, the more change we incite.

7. A substantial source of stress and sickness in the body is the lifelong repetition of negative ideas. Stress puts us in a "survival" mode, which badly affects our internal states and wears out our bodies. Consequently, negative reactions like rage, sadness, unhappiness, or confusion are produced. When we are in this mindset, it is comparable to acting like a prisoner or a bird in a cage because we are unable to perceive the possibilities for our lives. Because of their constant emotional state, which is a highly addictive byproduct of the release of neurochemicals, people become "stuck" in this way.

8. There are four main brain areas. The area of the brain responsible for decision-making, the frontal lobe, is the most changeable. Our "free will" is a function of the cerebral cortex or neocortex. 90% of the neurons in our brains are stored

in this region, which also controls information, attention, awareness, thoughts, language, and recordings of our knowledge and experiences. With the temporal lobe in charge of managing smell, sounds, speech, and vision, the parietal lobe processes sensory input.

9. Although studies show we are capable of making positive changes, our genes influence how we behave. The word "epigenetics," which refers to the influence of genetics on development, was coined by Conrad Waddington in 1942. Those who were effective in bringing about change educated themselves by reading, watching, and listening to motivational speakers to form fresh ideas and adopt new behaviors. Strong mind-body connections can be created by using visualization, a potent tool.

10. The ongoing loop of our thoughts and the chemical reactions taking place inside of us that produce our emotions make up our

state of being. This constant cycle directly affects our conduct.

11. To alter reality and restore physical health Making up our minds to do something is the key component. We can fully recover and alter our external circumstances in the same way that patients who were told they would never be able to walk again do so, athletes who sustain irreparable injuries do so but still go on to fully recover, or people who have been diagnosed with cancer and a few months later the disease is no longer detectable. They realize the key is having a strong intention, believing they can alter their circumstances, lots of grit, and the drive to manifest the life they want.

12. Knowledge acquisition and our life experiences are intertwined.
Our mind receives knowledge from the brain, while the body gives rise to our experiences in the mind.

"Knowledge without experience is philosophy, and experience without any knowledge is ignorance," Dispenza asserts to support this claim. Wisdom is created through the interaction of the two.

13. Intelligence to recognize the emergence of one's emotions is a result of lifelong learning, experiences, and conduct.
You must alter your state of mind to produce new feelings and ways of being to alter your existing reality.
No matter your genetic makeup, you can reinvent yourself. Make up your mind with utter confidence that you can achieve your goals by believing that you can.

Chapter 3

Focus on your needs in life

Being thcrc for your friends, devoting yourself to your job, and juggling a thousand different tasks is all part of the whirlwind that is life. It can be difficult to find time and concentrate on yourself with everything going on. When we talk about putting your needs first, we don't just mean taking a long, hot bath or spending one Sunday a month watching movies. By practicing self-inquiry, we mean taking regular breaks to check in with your emotions, adjust your goals, and ensure that you are doing more of the things you want to do in life and taking care of your own needs.

Why Self-Awareness Is Important

It may sound like an ego trip to focus on oneself, but that's far from the case. It makes us better people, both to ourselves and those around us. It enables us to advance, develop, set healthy boundaries, enhance our sense of well-being, and live a soul-intuned lifestyle. This Berkley article described a study in which it was discovered that participants were "happier when they had a balance of helping others and focusing on themselves too."

Self-improvement can seem overwhelming and large because it involves making significant changes or being clear on your life goals. This isn't always simple, especially after the profound cultural and lifestyle changes the pandemic has caused in all of us. There are various methods for learning how to concentrate on yourself. It may entail modest steps, long-lasting changes, and minor adjustments that keep you in control of your life. We can grow and thrive in our goals and mental health by staying in and outside of our comfort zones and avoiding complacency.

9 Techniques For Self-Awareness

Here are a few quick, easy tips to help you learn how to take care of yourself and make time in your schedule for introspection and thought.

1. Be Dedicated to Regular Health Checks

Sometimes the simplest things can make a difference in terms of self-improvement; it's not always about big-picture thinking and lofty goals.

Making ensuring your fundamental needs are addressed can be a good place to start when embracing self-love.

This is getting enough rest, staying hydrated, aiming for a simple workout regimen, inhaling plenty of fresh air, and overall keeping an eye on your physical body each day. A significant shift in thinking might result from taking these little but crucial actions.

Self-care and self-love are the cornerstones of motivation, and they can help you feel prepared to take on more challenging goals.

2. Stop Negative Self-Talk

Language matters. We all agree on this when it comes to talking to the people we care about in our lives, but we don't always practice it when it comes to ourselves. Regarding the thoughts that run amok in our minds, self-compassion is important as well.

We are aware that controlling negative thought patterns is not always simple, but being aware of how our inner dialogue is developing right now and understanding how our ideas make us feel, can be one of the most beneficial adjustments you make in your life. It's not always simple to learn to be kind to oneself, but it's the key to a lot happier existence. Take a look at this study to see how self-talk helps control our anxiety.

3. Keep in Mind That Micro Habits Count

Since we frequently start with the major ideas in our minds when discussing personal development, it can all feel extremely daunting. Are we content with our position, our relationship, or our current state of affairs?

These questions are significant, but they may be too intrusive for our mental health, causing us to become paralyzed or unable to see a clear path forward.

Micro habits can significantly alter behavior.

Each trip starts with a single step, and each transformation begins with a single second. One line in a gratitude notebook every evening, ten bucks saved each week, or five minutes of yoga in the morning can all help you feel more in control of your larger goals. These are good, actionable steps that help you reach your major objective.

4. Write in a Journal

It's not necessary to be a writer to gain much from keeping a journal. You can process your ideas, let go of anything you may have been holding onto, and better understand how you are feeling right now by making it a habit to write a few pages every day.

Some people claim that morning pages are the greatest because when our minds are less constrained, we naturally write and allow our genuine, unfiltered thoughts to come through—especially when we know that no one will see them. What comes out may surprise you.

The option to set aside time for yourself is another advantage of starting a journaling routine. Writing in a notebook for 10 minutes each day is a proactive way to spend ten minutes of your day reflecting on yourself and your views about life.

5. Pick a helpful hobby

Developing new interests is one of the finest ways to improve your sense of self.

A great approach to spend some of your free time doing what you enjoy is to engage in a hobby.

Studies have shown that hobbies, experiences, diverse interests, and new things may all be very helpful for reducing anxiety and addressing mental health issues, whether it's cold water swimming, learning a musical instrument, enrolling in a dance class, or taking a DIY class.

Having a pastime allows us to better get to know and comprehend who we are. Just be sure that the activity you choose is one that you genuinely want to do, rather than following someone else's lead or pursuing what you believe you ought to be doing.

6. Take Regular Breaks from Social Media

Instagram, TikTok, and Facebook can still steer us toward harmful habits and comparisons even if we are all aware that social media can be a smoke and mirrors act (most of us only share positive things). Regular social media breaks can help you break the scroll-and-compare cycle and keep you anchored in the real world.

Constantly updating social media may sometimes lead to disassociation or voyeuristic outsider perspectives on our own life. Because we view ourselves through the eyes of people who browse through our social media feeds, we may feel cut off from our conceptions of happiness, success, and healthy relationships.

Overuse of social media can exacerbate loneliness, increase FOMO, eat up a lot of free time that could be spent taking proactive steps for your well-being, and keep you grounded or trapped in the past. While we don't advocate deleting all of your social media apps, taking regular breaks can be incredibly liberating.

7. Employ reliable coping mechanisms

It never hurts to have a coping strategy plan in place because life loves to throw curveballs our way, whether it be a terrible day at work, a breakup in your relationship, the stress of having too many obligations, or anything else that drives you over the brink.

Knowing oneself better involves discovering what works for you when times are difficult. To help you focus or change your energy when you are experiencing emotional overwhelm, try meditation or exercise. It might be developing healthy boundaries by practicing saying "no" to little things around others who can offer you a safe environment to do so. Going for a walk could help you when you're feeling anxious or easily irritated. It might be soliciting assistance with tasks or honing communication abilities.

One of the most significant gifts you can offer yourself is a solid understanding of coping mechanisms since it affirms your self-confidence and empowers you to make decisions that will improve your well-being.

It enhances self-esteem, lessens codependency, and generally makes day-to-day living seem more manageable.

8. Turn Your Attention inward

For individuals who need to be embodied and connected, regularly checking in with themselves is a smart idea.

It can be simple to let others set our goals for us and adhere to their concept of happiness. Reorienting your attention to yourself and deciding how you want your life to entail learning how to focus on yourself.

Reaching our deepest aspirations entails connecting with the experiences that make us feel fulfilled, alive, and enthusiastic. It entails mastering the ability to put internal distractions aside and examining all the various facets of your life and yourself to determine what feels comfortable and what is too restrictive. We are better able to make decisions that support our sense of self as we become more aware of and in tune with ourselves.

This practice entails just pausing when someone speaks or anything occurs to shift into your own body and thoughts and assess how it feels. Somatic decision-making keeps us grounded in our bodies while developing our capacity to make decisions based on intuition.

9. Compile a Very Long Dream List.

Make a list of all the goals you have for your life and the issues that are important to you. Not a top ten list, but a lengthy, sprawling list with 200 bullet points is what we're referring to. Wait until the end before reading the list back as you go through it to make it.

When you reach 200 items and reread it, you could observe that several similar or the same item again appears. By doing this, you can discover what is essential to you, what lies beneath the noise, what is continually awaiting in the subconscious, and what you want to accomplish with your one wild and precious life.

Not only will spending time on your ambitions and wishes provide you the opportunity to spend time alone with your ideas for the future, but it will also enable you to become organized, clarify your goals for the future, and create a life that perfectly matches your needs.

How can you briefly go away from the outside world to bring your attention back to yourself? Do you believe that having aspirations and desires is essential in the long run? I

Chapter 4

Stop chasing the next thing focus on what matters

Whenever we run after anything, we pull ourselves out of the present moment when life genuinely occurs. The future doesn't exist yet and the past is gone. The only genuinely significant place to live is in the present and that's typically where you'll find what you're searching for.

Pursuing the next thing implies, chasing what does not significant to you or bettering your life to another level.

Here are 5 things to quit chasing:

- **Stop Chasing Security**

"In this life, nothing can be considered to be certain, except death and taxes." ~ Benjamin Franklin

According to the Merriam-Webster definition, security is "the condition of being protected or secure from harm." The trouble with seeking security is that there is no such thing, and if you exchange your soul for it, you pay a hefty price. I have a guy who's purchasing a home with a lady he doesn't love, who treats him poorly, for "security's sake." Another acquaintance is looking for employment well under her potential to receive a stable salary, even though the last time she did so her job made her ill and it pulled her out of the job market for many months.

The fact is that fear of change and sticking in our comfort zones slows our progress. Each of us has a distinct mission in life. Most of us don't recognize it, however, because we've been driven to conform to someone else's image of who we should be. Stretch yourself and take a risk if you want to find out what makes your heart sing.

- **Stop Chasing Money**

"Chase your interests and money will come. Chase money and you may never discover your passions." ~ Colin Wright

We all need to make ends meet, but beyond that, chasing after the green stuff doesn't make us happy.

The error most individuals make in the quest for success is seeking money. This makes sense since it appears like the best thing to do when you are facing a shortage. But this theory explains why most of the world is broke, they are claiming they don't have enough, and therefore consequently, they DON'T have enough.

It's like chasing a butterfly. It would always elude you. You have to expand your inner ability as a person, and the money that you are worth would be ATTRACTED to you. There has to be a foundation laid, because if you create it too soon, you're not ready for it, and you may lose it just as fast if not faster.

Listen, the money that you have constantly rises or falls to your degree of inner potential. Give a poor guy $1 million now, and sooner or later, that money would plummet to the level of his inner ability. It's typically only a question of time. I'm sure you've observed this with lottery winners, 70% end up filing for bankruptcy or the Sport betting men who waste all their earnings on frivolities!

So, you have to concentrate on the proper things. Focus on yourself, invest in yourself. That's where all the magic occurs that's what has the most influence on your revenue. Not your parents, not your upbringing, not the economy..... You.

In increasing capacity, here's a simple formula that if you regularly apply, your inner capacity will undoubtedly expand.

Learn + Do = Become.

- **Stop Chasing Material Things**

"Stop pursuing what your mind wants and you'll obtain what your soul needs." ~ KushandWizdom

"You only live once, but if you do it correctly, once is enough." – Mae West

There is greater satisfaction in chasing less than can be found in pursuing more. In many respects, this is a message that we already know to be true.

It's only that, from the day we were born, we have been taught something else. We have been taught that goods equal pleasure. And because we have heard that message so many times and from so many perspectives, we have come to believe it. As a consequence, we spend our lives working long hours to get excellent money so that we may acquire lovely items.

But when we again hear the simple message that there is more joy in pursuing less than can be found in pursuing more, it rings true in our hearts... because deep down, we already know it to be true. We know that things don't equal pleasure. And we realize that our life is much too important to squander following them.

It simply helps to be reminded from time to time. So today, remember...
Our life is brief. We only get one chance at it. Time flies by rapidly. And once we use it up, we can't get it back. So make the most of it. Possessions rob our time and energy. They need constant upkeep to be cleaned, maintained, mended, replaced and removed. They take our valuable attention, time, and energy and we don't even realize it... until it's too late.

Our life is unique. Our appearance, our personality, our abilities, and the individuals who have affected our life have made us distinctive. As a consequence, our life is precisely like no one else. And just because everyone else is seeking material stuff doesn't mean we have to too.

Our life is important. Far more than achievement, our souls crave meaning because significance lasts forever. On the other hand, possessions are temporary. They decay, spoil, and fade. And most of them, by design.

Our life is made to inspire. Let's build footsteps worth following. Nobody ever changed the world by following someone else. Instead, those who transform the world live differently and encourage others to do the same. Possessions may superficially dazzle, but they never inspire.

Our life is important. Our hearts and soul make us valuable. Don't abandon your crucial function in this world by settling for items that can be bought with a card of plastic.

Our life deserves better. Joy, happiness, and contentment are found in the unseen things of life: love, hope, peace, and connections. And they are not for sale at your local department store. Stop searching for them there. People who dedicate their lives to chase of stuff are never fulfilled. They constantly seek newer, quicker, or greater since worldly items will never fulfill our innermost heart needs.

Be reminded that your life is much too important to squander pursuing material stuff. And discover greater delight today by choosing to seek "better," rather than "more."

- **Stop Chasing Outer Beauty**

The stress of appearing nice on the exterior may take a toll on the insides Beauty. It is captivating, powerful, puzzling, changing, and absorbing.

Everyone has a distinct concept of and connection with this driving force of self-image and social interaction. Psychologists and behaviorists argue the urge to be attractive is firmly rooted in both our psychology and biology. It motivates our reproductive desires and shapes our feeling of self-confidence and social stature. As a consequence, people have struggled for generations to beautify themselves on the surface.

Many could suggest that aspects of conduct and personal values (i.e., compassion, kindness, and generosity) better explain the genuine meaning of beauty. But if beauty is essentially a result of spirit and personality, why do we allow physical looks to affect so much of our behavior and values?..

“For lovely eyes, search for the good in others. For beautiful lips, utter only words of compassion; and for poise, walk with the certainty that you are never alone." ~ Audrey Hepburn

Many women and men feel pressure to appear nice. We go to the gym, color our hair, and even seek corrective surgery. In 2012, 14.6 million cosmetic treatments were done in the United States. Isabella Rossellini calls it "the new foot binding." The difficulty is that exterior beauty naturally diminishes with time. What we should be seeking is the beauty that exists inside.

- **Stop Chasing Approval**

"Always remember that you do not need to explain yourself or prove anything to anybody. If they cannot accept you for you - then it is time to move on." ~ Cath B Akesson

After people's acceptance is a waste of time and effort; what we should be chasing is our approval. The third regret of the dying is that they wish they'd had the bravery to communicate their actual sentiments instead of bottling their emotions down to preserve peace with others.

There's NOTHING wrong with you. Others individuals adore you exactly the way you are; some don't. You don't need to alter a thing. The great side effect of self-acceptance is that the minor things you desire to change about yourself tend to correct themselves naturally. Self-hate keeps you trapped. Self-acceptance heals.

Reasons to Stop pursuing Approval

Here are some core reasons that may drive you to undertake a necessary journey to be your own best friend. The invitation is before each one of us: "Don't be polite, be genuine!

Peace rises when we pick ourselves and what's essential to us.

The more we identify with what matters to us, the happier we become.
It's possible to be compassionate and not be a people pleaser.
When we live by our truth and values instead of seeking acceptance, confidence blooms, and there are ease and flow.
Immense freedom arises when we are embraced for who we are.

What Matters - The 7 Most Important Things in Life

Life is fleeting and in a world of turmoil, social media, and conflict, priceless things may quickly get forgotten. Occasionally, events beyond our control cause loss, and sometimes our actions lead us to lose the things that matter the most. We all have various wants and priorities in life, but we have one thing in common: the lack of some things in life leads us to feel incomplete. While our lives and priorities may vary, there are certain things crucial to living a life of fulfillment... things we need to strive for...

things that matter. Never lose sight of these 7 crucial things in life.

Peace Rule #1, defend your peace. I used to get highly impacted by my environment. If my environment was bad, I had to fight hard not to spiral into a negative attitude. The reality is, that life isn't simple, and living in our quaint comfort zones doesn't open the window for change. The more confidence you become in the love you have for yourself, the more you recognize that you are strong enough to walk in a place where the tension is intense and preserve your serenity.

When you safeguard your tranquility, you can then balance your emotions and handle relationships and difficult circumstances efficiently. This can help you build self-confidence and come to terms with yourself so that you may reach inner peace and nurture a more positive attitude towards life.

Do yourself a life-changing favor and love yourself enough to put your peace first; love yourself enough to indulge yourself. This is not selfish, it is self-preservation and self-love. You don't deserve to feel "less than." You don't have to measure up to the expectations people impose on you. Love yourself enough to defend your tranquility.

Health

So many of us take our health for granted until something life-changing occurs, and our health becomes at stake. With excellent health, everything is possible. Without it, you cannot experience life to its utmost. It is crucial to take care of your mind, body, and spirit. Pay heed to what your body is telling you. Take charge of your whole health. Eat properly and exercise frequently to decrease preventable diseases and the stress that may be stopping you from enjoying life.

Focus on your health and remember to exercise self-care. Though we may be caretakers or breadwinners for others, we need to concentrate on our health – and mental health. In reality, the more we can care for our well-being, the more prepared we are to be of service to others.

Being more present, eating healthily, and finding time to unwind can increase your mental health and general well-being. Practice being nicer to yourself by taking time to refresh yourself mentally and focus on all areas of your health.

Family & Friendship

Our connections are our basis. They are certainly the things that make our life richer and more complete. We must prioritize time with friends, family, and loved ones to build our connections. Being busy is natural, but why not attempt to be busy with the people who matter the most to us?

Having individuals in your life who you can name family is invaluable. Knowing that you have someone who cares for you and will always be there for you is the sort of support we all need, even if we don't always acknowledge it. But it is so easy to overlook exactly how much family matters to us. They're the individuals we normally take for granted because, at the end of the day, we know they will still be family. Always remember, your family is irreplaceable. You must commit time, love, and energy to develop your family ties — not only for the benefit of your family but for yourself.

You can't choose your family, but you can choose your friends and make them members of your family. If you know a person you can call your best friend, then consider yourself fortunate. Make the most out of your time with your friends and, more importantly, be the greatest friend you can be.

The unconditional love of family is an incredible sensation and while you may not always see eye-to-eye, accept each other's individuality and try your best to demonstrate your affection more frequently.

Purpose

The purpose is our "why." It drives our every action and fuels our passion. It covers our careers, our relationships, and our attitude to living our best lives. Our mission wraps around everything we do in our life. To live a meaningful life, we must have a purpose - a goal, an objective we wish to reach while we walk this Earth. I feel like I truly started living when I found my purpose. It's a never-ending quest that I wake up enthusiastic about every single day. You may call it your ambitions, job aspirations, or your notion of success, but if you truly want to make a difference in this world, you have to begin with yourself. So, delve deep to find out what you're passionate about and how that passion may have a good influence on people around you, then go after it with zeal for the rest of your life. It implies purposefully living your life. Ultimately, it becomes your legacy.

Time

Time is a scarce resource; once it is wasted, it's gone forever. We cannot ever get time back, but we can be intentional with the time that we have.

We all have the same number of hours in our day, hours that are filled with responsibilities and obligations. Managing time frequently boils down to decisions. The trouble is, we say "yes" much too frequently. This is when we lose equilibrium. Each time we say "yes" to something, we are saying "no" to something else. Instead of feeling in control of our schedule, we feel our time is not our own. We run from one obligation to the next, never feeling completely present at any of them. We squeeze more into our days yet feel we have less and less time to accomplish the things we truly want to do or to see the people we want to see. We have less room left for ourselves.

We can take control by saying "yes" to less and appreciating the blank space in our diary. We can protect our precious time, saving it for the activities and people that give our lives the most meaning and joy.

Learning

Life is a gift and we must make the most of it. You must constantly spend on increasing your knowledge and abilities. One day I believe I am an expert in a subject, and the following day I am presented with a challenge that teaches me differently. It is to our advantage to treat adversities as a learning opportunity. Discover and nurture your gifts via continual study and you will add enormous depth and purpose to your life.

I made a very intentional choice to go back to school to get my Ph.D. this autumn. Though extremely encouraging, I had mentors and coworkers advise me that to attain my job objectives, going back to school was unnecessary. Though it may be true, my persistent drive to study has pushed me on this road. I thought that expanding my mind to new notions in education and pairing that science with my expertise was too intriguing to pass up. As B.B. King so eloquently stated, "The beautiful thing about learning is that nobody can take it away from you."

Our human value transcends formal schooling and professional growth, of course. It is a total of all we encounter, achieve, confront, and conquer. The more you broaden your learning, the more useful you become.

Love

I have always maintained, that we were here on this world only to love. Love one another, love what we do, enjoy the Earth and love each moment we are privileged to experience. Love is the most powerful force in the universe.

The actual mark of greatness is displayed via love's gestures of kindness, compassion, helpfulness, and care. Even if you don't love your life itself, via loving things or people in your life you may still discover meaning and purpose.

Learning how to enjoy your position in the world helps establish a good, healthy attitude toward life. Through love, we receive understanding, mercy, joy, and forgiveness. Through love, most of our emotional requirements are addressed. Through love, we feel deserving and valid. Through love, we serve a greater cause and join in a higher calling.

The energy of love is the greatest energy we can feel and actions of love enhance our awareness of the world. Our capacity to approach the world with love creates an example for others to strive for while teaching compassion, forgiveness, tolerance, and peace.

Just picture a world where every action is anchored on love. I know I do!

Chapter 5

Give up on what does not matter.

Sometimes, giving up some things is all that is necessary to achieve success and move closer to the person we can become. Even if every one of us may have a different notion of success, some things are universal and will help you succeed if you give up on them.

Some of these you can give up on right now, while others might require a little more time.

1. Put an end to your unhealthy lifestyle

"Look after your body. You are required to live there only." [Jim Rohn]

Everything begins here if you want to succeed in life. There are only two things you need to keep in mind when caring for your health first:

i. Healthy Eating
ii. Physical Activity
You'll one day be grateful you took even small steps.

2. **Give up having a limited perspective**.
"If you live life well, once is plenty. You only live once." [Mae West]
Successful people set long-term objectives, but they are aware that these objectives are only the result of daily, short-term behaviors.
You should not just practice these healthy habits; you should live them.
The phrases "working out to acquire a summer body" and "working out because that's who you are" are not interchangeable.

3. **Stop trying to be too modest.**
"The world is not served by you acting small. Shrinkage for the sake of making others feel

more at ease around you is not enlightened. We're all supposed to shine, just like kids do. Everyone has it; it is not unique to any of us. As we let our light shine, we unintentionally offer others permission to do the same. Our presence naturally liberates others as we are liberated from our anxiety."
[Marianne Williamson]
Your complete potential can never be realized if you never make an effort to seize excellent possibilities or let your aspirations come true.
And what you could have accomplished will never be useful to the world.
Don't be scared to express your thoughts, to fail, and certainly not to succeed.

4. Drop the justifications.
The way you play the hand, not the cards you're given, is what matters.
From Randy Pausch's The Last Lecture

Regardless of their starting place, flaws, or prior failures, successful people are aware that they are ultimately responsible for their lives. It's both frightful and exciting to understand that you are in charge of what occurs next in your life.
And once you do, it becomes impossible for you to fail because justifications restrict and prohibit us from developing both emotionally and professionally. No one else will own your life; you must.

5. Let go of the rigid perspective

"Those who learn additional skills and mix them in original ways will own the future." The Mastery of Robert Greene
People who have a fixed mindset think their intelligence or talents are just fixed traits, and they believe talent alone can bring about success without any other factors. They're in error.
Effective people are aware of this. They devote a significant amount of time each day

to cultivating a growth mindset, learning new things, gaining new abilities, and altering their perspectives to improve their life.
Never forget that who you are today is not always who you must be tomorrow.

6. Stop relying on "the magic bullet"
"I'm growing better and better every day in every aspect," you say. (Émile Coué)

Success appears overnight as a myth. Successful people understand that daily tiny improvements add up over time and will produce the desired outcomes.
Because of this, you should make plans for the future while concentrating on the day that is right in front of you. Aim to make just 1% progress every day.

7. Let go of perfectionism
Perfection is beaten by shipping. Kahn Academy's Development Mantra

No matter how hard we try, nothing will ever be flawless.
Our inability to act and release our invention into the world is frequently due to our fear of failure (or even success). However, if we wait for everything to be perfect, we risk missing out on a lot of possibilities.
To improve (that 1%), "ship," and then improve.

8. Quit multitasking

If you stop and hurl rocks at each barking dog, you'll never get where you're going. Churchill, Winston S.
Effective people are aware of this. They pick a single object and subdue it for this reason. Whatever it is, whether a business concept, a chat, or a workout.
It is essential to be fully present and focused on one task.

9. Let go of the need to be in charge of everything

"Some things are in our control, and some things are not in our control." – Epictetus, a Stoic thinker

It's crucial to distinguish between these two. Recognize that sometimes the only thing you will be able to manage is your attitude toward something, and separate yourself from the things you cannot control and concentrate on the ones you can.

Keep in mind that no one can be annoyed while yelling "Bubbles" angrily.

10. Stop accepting offers that don't advance your objectives.

"He who wants to achieve little must give little; he who wants to achieve much must give more; he who wants to obtain highly must give much." James Allen

Successful people understand that to achieve their goals, they will need to refuse

certain requests from their friends, family, and coworkers.
You might give up some short-term pleasure now, but it will all be worthwhile if your goals are achieved.

11. Let go of the negative people

The five individuals you spend the most time with define you as a whole. Mr. Jim Rohn
Who we become is influenced by the people we spend the most time with. In both their personal and professional lives, some are less accomplished than us, and vice versa. Your success will decrease if you spend time with those who are behind you in the class; this will also lower your average.
But no matter how difficult it may be, you will succeed if you spend time with people who are more successful than you.
See if you need to make any adjustments by taking a glance at yourself.

12. Let go of your need to be popular

"Not doing anything significant is the only surefire method to keep people happy." [Oliver Emberton]

Consider your identity as a market niche.

There will be a sizable number of people who enjoy that specialty and some who don't. And no matter what you try, the market won't accept you as the only option.

No need to defend yourself—this is very normal.

The only thing you can do is be true to yourself, constantly strive to be better and add value, and understand that the increasing number of "haters" is a sign of your success.

13. Stop relying on social media and television.

You assume you have time, which is the problem.

— Jack Kornfield

The diseases of modern civilization are impulsive online browsing and television viewing. Never allow these two to serve as a diversion from your life or your objectives.

If neither is necessary to achieve your goals, you should reduce (or possibly do away with) your reliance on them and devote that time to activities that would improve your life.

www.ingramcontent.com/pod-product-compliance
Lightning Source LLC
LaVergne TN
LVHW050344160826
845677LV00014B/3787